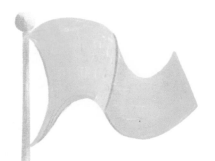

Dedicated to the loving memory of Tim "Buck" Myers.

The only thing our dad loved more than golf was his wife, 6 kids and 7 grandkids. Buck taught us to love the game. Some of us are good at it, some not so much. But what we learned from our dad was... "You don't need to be good to have fun."

Timothy's Tee Time

Written by
Teddy Myers and Timmy Myers

Illustrated by
Katie Stack

On a golf course off old 494,
    there was a little boy named Timothy
      who had never played golf before.

The other kids said,
"If you don't have clubs, you can't play this round."
So he decided to go check the lost and found.

He searched

and he searched,

then he heard someone shout...

In a shed next to some rakes and a rusty water spout,
was an old set of golf clubs that had all but been forgotten about.

As Timothy got closer,
he couldn't believe his eyes.
That old set of clubs...
they were alive!

"We haven't played in years."

Timothy told them, "We don't need to be good, we can just have fun.
And maybe we'll learn a thing or two by the time we are done."

In the bag he found a ball and a tee.

"This guy is pushy."

"You're telling me."

"I'm the driver. Swing me with all your might.
Just be sure to watch out for the water on the right."

With a loud **whack**
things quickly started to look grim.

"I forgot to mention this
but um... I CAN'T SWIM!"

To get the ball on the green, use one of the irons, 7, 8, or 9.
"We're brothers and sisters, so we don't get along all the time."

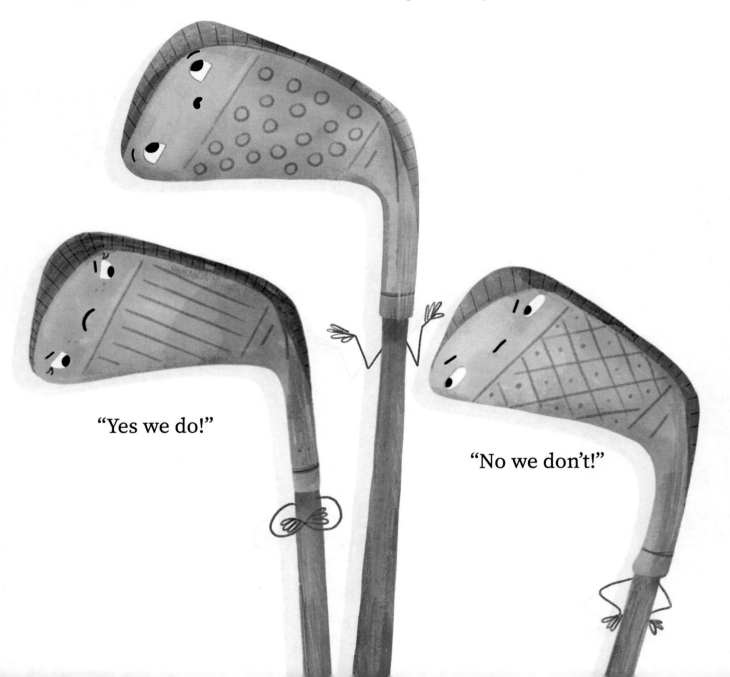

"Yes we do!"

"No we don't!"

Whatever you do,
don't choose wrong.

Otherwise you'll hit the ball
too short or too long.

You'll need the soft touch of the wedge to get it close to the cup.

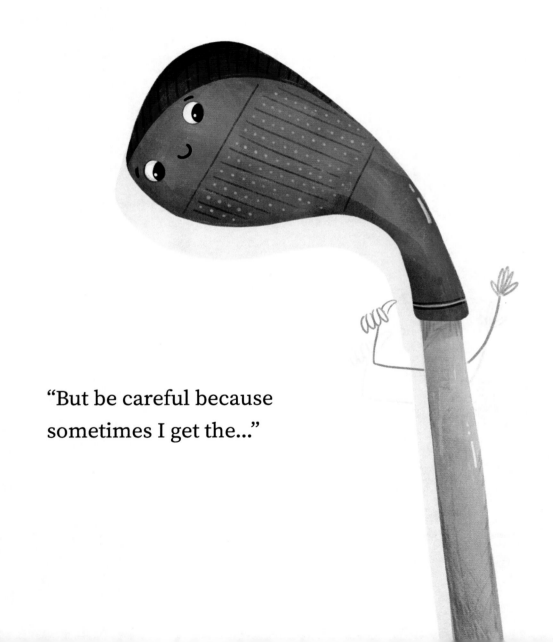

"But be careful because
sometimes I get the..."

Now that we're on the green, it's time to make it roll.

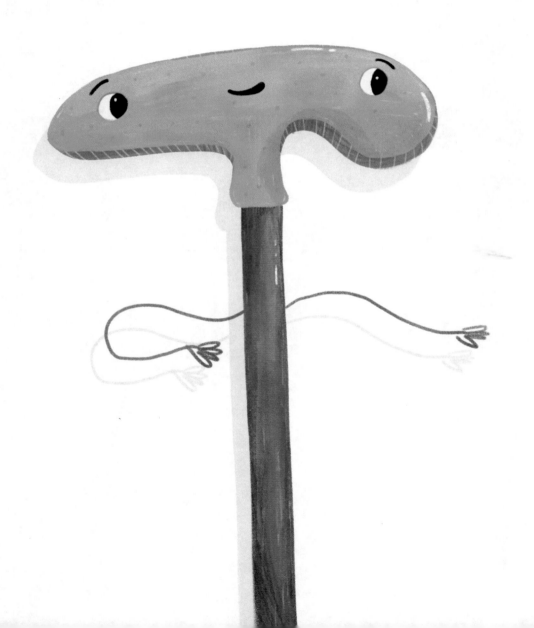

"Use me, the putter, to get the ball in the..."

"in the..."

"in the hole!"

The clubs were upset that their play was so bad.

Then Timothy came over and said,
"This is the most fun I've ever had!"

That's when they realized, you don't need to be good to have fun.
And maybe you can learn a thing or two by the time you are done.

So the driver swung hard but with a little more grace.
And Timothy promised not to put that stinky sock back on his face.

The wedge was able to
keep his hiccups at bay.

And on the last hole, the putter made it in from a long, long way.

As the ball rolled in, a red cart rolled near.
It was a good-looking man with some gray in his beard.

"Nice putt," he said.
"I think you
found my clubs."

"They work better
for you,
keep 'em bud."

And just like that, the nice man drove away,
the perfect end to the perfect day.

Made in United States
North Haven, CT
24 April 2024

51709088R00020